if walls could whisper

Ola Soszynski

BookLeaf
Publishing

India | USA | UK

Presentation by *BookLeaf Publishing*

Web: www.bookleafpub.com

E-mail: info@bookleafpub.com

ISBN: 9789358361797

First edition 2021

For all the people who supported me along the way, and the ordinary friends found in odd places.

I love you all.

And so it begins.
    My palms sweat against the concrete fingertips
    longing to touch anyone else I press harder;
        and harder still.
Rocks may dig into my skin.
    Cut my hands
    but it will not be enough.
    I trace the surface
        and prepare the fall.
How long has it been
    since I took a risk like this?

Will you recognize me
            when it's over?
You do not surprise me anymore.
    Now, I can simply turn around
        and know you'll be there;
    waiting, joking.
We are not in love.
 promise.
    This is a different sort.
        The kind that leaves me burning,
    bruised and cared for.

You know me too well.
       I cannot love you.
       We made a promise.
I can still love
       But I do not love you.
          In the lazy days
          the kicked covers
               the frustration and curiosity
                I promised.
I should not love you.
                I will not.

                  I promise.
It is in the sun
       that I miss those rainy days the most. The
earth shaking,
       the plunge into darkness.
Candlelight and cold showers
       to prepare for rest.
Call me odd.
       Call me anything you'd like.
But in the end

you will find me there,

Smiling up at rainclouds

and hoping it never ends
They always come to me.

Broken glass to superglue.

I think they trust me.

But I can only pretend to help

say the words I know they want to hear; The

things I wish I had been told.

I try my best to mend them:

lay out the pieces,

describe the process.

But I always get glue on my fingers. My

hands, they stick together,

and I fumble to act as though

it was intended.

All is well.

Simply shove me under scalding water, or

leave it to freeze with time.

Dull the burn, the cracks, the bond.

Rip the remnants from me.

These half-truths are all I can offer.
My hands come undone

and I can hand you

your somewhat repaired self.

Do not look behind me.

There are shards of glass

caught in my floorboards,

swept under the rug.

Hurting me with every step

from self-inflicted projects

I could never fix.

Thank you for visiting.

I'm glad I could help.

Please come again.

Clarity has never been easy.

Something in the way we talk

changed.

Necessary, but unwelcome

I wish we could go back

to rose-tinted ignorance.

But instead we lay,

unfiltered, unfinished.

Undone.

Can we just bandage the break?

Ignore the signs,

and act like nothing happened?

I've never wanted to pretend harder than

now

than with you sat there.

Please leave me to my thoughts.

Let me remember.

Let me pretend.

It's in the silences

that I realize

I have changed.

The way I see the sky

as it ever-shifts

and the morning just begins to wake. In my

lonesome,

staring at ceilings

and thinking about nothing at all

I can notice

the world

moving around me.

But I do not know

if it is better

or worse.

For a Stranger

What is it you think about,

those lonely nights?

What lingers on your tongue

in the poisonous silence?

Where does your mind drift to

when all the world falls away?

Do you ever try to hold the sky?

Palms raised, ready for the burden

that never seems to arrive?

Do you struggle to rest, like me?

Does the world on pause

have you wish it could last forever?

When do your eyes

begin to win

against the desire to peer into the unknown? And

when you hear the morning's songs, are you happy?

I hope you're happy.

would like to believe

that as the day pours on,

we collect fragments

of how moments felt.

Or rather;

that they get caught.

Snagged within

our backpacks, knapsacks,

our pockets and purses.

So once we arrive at the end of the day as we

detach, undress

from the world around us

these pieces come together,

and are released.

Just before midnight.
The world ended around me.

Cracking.

Crumbling.

Collapsing.

Overwhelmed, I saw no choice.

So, I stayed.

I stayed

and waited for it to end.

I'm tired of waiting.

The world will not end fast enough, and I

am stronger than I let myself see. I am

capable

of rebuilding

of planning

of trying.

The world is still ending.

It always will be.

Slowly.

Slowly.

Piece by piece

    I will rust from the inside out. But for

    now

    I am here.

I am here

    and I will be here

    waiting for the world to end and

    when it does

I will show it all I made.
Coffee cups

    and small talk.

    This is how it ends.

Woefully domestic.

    Passion caged and trained

    to be convenient.

The dishes left in the sink

    overflow

    and we work once more.

I will not let myself be

    overwhelmed.

    Not quite one step at a time. Wave

by wave.

      Notes taped to the wall

      serve as reminders.

Expectations.

      Keep me grounded

      in the moment of chaos.

In moments of life,

      they remind the wild

      of the calm.

Do you think death forgets? Looks at

            time,

      then at you,

      and asks

         "Oh, you're still here?"

            On Death

Death is a close friend of mine.

      Someone I greet every so often

      but never invite inside.

Death is the acquaintance

      I see down the street,

with a simple smile and nod of hello.

I wish we were closer.
	That we could lay and watch the sky and tell
	them my dreams
	but I know they'd only laugh;
I should know better than that, after all.

They would never force me.
	Death does not drag anyone by the wrist to do
	anything unwanted;
			they hold your hand gently,
			waiting until you're ready.
Death doesn't cling.
	They're rather the opposite,
	because no matter how many others we **see**, we
	can laugh.

For we know,
	regardless of how many
	come between us,

we'll end up together.
                    Broken Bike Parts

She says he did it
        long ago.
Saw his broken parts,
        and traded out the tires in secret
                    leaving us ever deflated.

Air escapes our lungs
        but we know nothing else.
                    Destroy ourselves at the best times.

She refuses to ride again.
        She fell too many times.
        Chains cut deep across her leg
        and she refuses to let go
            of the memory.
We blame the pump
        for not filling the void properly
        for fixing everyone else fine

            for not telling us sooner.

t lays,

    dusted and deflated

    another took its place.

            Perhaps I'll go on a ride today.

What a tragedy

    to so fully

    convince yourself

        of the inability to love.

To see the world;

    its pain and hurt

    and decide you couldn't

        unless allowed.

Relearn the innocent bliss

    of yelling from the rooftops.

See the beauty in the mundane

    and proclaim to the world:

I love

     I love.

          I love!

               I will not let this be taken away
I can't help but wonder

     about my expiration date.

What if my "best by" is long past the thoughts &

     feelings crumbs?

Would you cut past the stale?

     The brittle and rotten?

Is there any me left?

     Please let me know
It curls

     up and around

          my heart.
An almost constant.

     An almost comfort.

An always.

It grabs at me

forces me to listen

as it bares its claws.

Further

and

further.

I need to put it down.

To sleep.

To explore.

But at this point

it might have buried itself so deep.

I do not know

where it starts

and where I begin.

Please do not dream of me.

Do not see me

outside of my control

Dreams are unpredictable.

Ideal.

Not I.
I fell for you.

so hard

that dust

became my oxygen.

and I'm not certain

that I want to stand.
Can we just exist?

Here?

Now?

My soul saw yours

and I don't want to go.
Her bedroom door sometimes shudders. As though for

a brief moment of the day It realizes its fate.

Bolted to the wall

Forced to watch,

to shield.

To shut off the world.

She shudders, sometimes.

As though she's noticed

The futility of it all.

But she manages.

Perhaps it's the weight of the air.

                            the heat.

Or maybe,

        these shudders

        are our way of saying

                see me

                notice me

I am here

        I am still here.
Words thrown

        out and into

                abyss.

Surely this can't be it.

        No, not yet.

                I refuse to end here.

These words

        shall travel

                past me

and onto whoever

        they are meant for.